ROBERT BURNS "WOMEN"
TWELVE WORKS INSPIRED BY WOMEN

ALASTAIR TURNBULL

Contents

Introduction 1
Handsome Nell 5
The Lass O' Cessnock Banks 12
Rigs O' Barley 21
The Lass O' Ballochmyle 28
To Mary in Heaven 34
Ae fond Kiss 40
I Love my Jean 47
Beware O' Bonie Ann 52
The Gowden Locks of Anna 55
The Bonnie Wee Thing 61
The Rights of a Woman 66
Lovely Young Jessie 73
Glossary 78
About the Author 138
Also by Alastair Turnbull 141

Big Red Resources

All text, except the words of Robert Burns, Copyright © 2016 by Alastair Turnbull

All rights reserved.

No part of this book may be reproduced in any form or by any electronic or mechanical means, including information storage and retrieval systems, without written permission from the author, except for the use of brief quotations.

INTRODUCTION

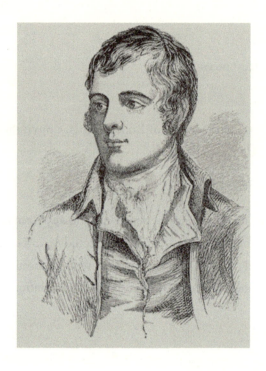

Robert Burns was born on the 25th of January 1759, the first son of William and Agnes Burnes. He was born into what we would now call "abject poverty", but his family was hard working and his father believed in education. Robert, along with his brothers and sisters, was given a tutor. They were tutored in the evening, after they had finished working on the farm during the day.

Robert grew up working hard on the land and reading avidly. He gained a great interest in poems and songs from his mother and his aunt, who were both well known for singing old Scots songs and retelling old Scottish tales. He first picked up the quill and wrote when he was just 15 years old. The subject of this poem was a girl, 'handsome Nell'. This innocent, but inspirational gesture was the first of many poems about women that Robert would write in his lifetime.

Robert's writing talents grew and eventually a book of his poems was published in 1786 called, "Poems Chiefly in the Scottish Dialect". This lead to him becoming the 18th century equivalent of a "celebrity" and he moved to Edinburgh with the aim of producing a second volume of poems.

Robert's life then became more complicated than that of a mere tenant farmer from Ayr. He mixed with the great and the good from Edinburgh society, joined drinking and debating clubs, travelled all over Scotland and was welcomed in many stately homes. At the same time as this he was courting Jean

Armour, (a girl he met in Mauchline), was a father to at least three children and his family were suffering hardship trying to farm and make ends meet.

Later in life Robert left farming, mainly due to ill health, and the fact that it was very hard work with little reward. He became an excise man and moved to Dumfries, taking his wife and family with him. He continued to write poetry and collect songs throught his lifetime.

Robert Burns died on the 21st July 1796.

The name of 'Robert Burns' means different things to different people. The majority will remember poems such as "My love is like a red, red rose", "Ae fond kiss" and "Tam O' Shanter". This will conjure up images of flowers, lovers, rural Scottish landscapes and mystical beings. This is the image of Scotland's "Ploughman poet", which is only one side of Robert Burns.

There are many other aspects to Robert Burns, such as Burns the Radical; he spoke out against the hypocrisy of the church and the injustice of the class system. Burns the Revolutionary; he supported the

French Revolution and the American War of Independence - both of which happened during his lifetime. Burns the Scotsman; he was fiercely proud of Scotland and a Jacobite sympathiser.

The aspect of Robert Burns that we are looking at in this book is his love of women. We will look at 12 works written by Robert, the women who inspired them and the types of relationship he had with those women. There are also modern English translations of the poems, these translations are here purely as an aid to understanding what is being said in the original poems, as the old Scots dialect Burns used in can be difficult to understand.

1
HANDSOME NELL

Handsome Nell was the first poem written by Robert Burns. He was just 15 years old and was working on his fathers rented farm, Mount Oliphant, which was about three miles outside of the town of Ayr. During the summer Robert's father, William, had hired some extra help to gather in the harvest, the custom at the time was to pair a male worker and a female worker together, one for physical strength and the other for better hand skills.

Who was Handsome Nell..?

Robert was paired with Nelly Kilpatrick, (Nelly is a nickname for Helen). Helen Kilpatrick was the 14-year-old daughter of John and Jane Kilpatrick, the local millers who ran the Perclewan Mill which was near the small town of Dalrymple.

This poem was unpublished in his lifetime but was included in his "Commonplace Book" and was set to Nelly's favourite reel, (unfortunately we don't know which reel that is). It is also part of the "Stair manuscripts collection", a group of eight songs and poems copied by Burns and sent to Mrs Alexander Stewart of Stair in 1786. These manuscripts are now held in the Burns Museum in Alloway.

Many years later Robert wrote a letter to Dr. Hunter, in the letter he talks about Nelly:
"Indeed, I did not well know myself I liked so much to loiter behind with her when returning in the evening from our labours; why the tones of her voice made my heart–strings thrill like an Aeolian harp, and particularly why my pulse beat such a furious rantann when I looked and fingered over her hand to pick out the nettle-stings and thistles".

Handsome Nell
    By Robert Burns
    Written: 1774
    Type: Poem & Song
    Tune: I am a man unmarried

Once I lov'd a bonie lass,
    Ay, and I love her still;
    And whilst that virtue warms my breast,

I'll love my handsome Nell.

As bonie lasses I have seen,
    And mony full as braw;
    But, for a modest gracefu' mein,
    The like I never saw.

A bonie lass, I will confess,
    Is pleasant to the e'e;
    But, without some better qualities,
    She's no a lass for me.

But Nelly's looks are blythe and sweet,
    And what is best of a',
    Her reputation is complete,
    And fair without a flaw.

She dresses aye sae clean and neat,
    Both decent and genteel;
    And there's something in her gait
    Gars ony dress look weel

A gaudy dress and gentle air

May slightly touch the heart;
But it's innocence and modesty
That polishes the dart.

'Tis this in Nelly pleases me,
   'Tis this enchants my soul;
   For absolutely in my breast
   She reigns without control.

Handsome Nell
   Translation

Once I loved a beautiful girl,
   And yes, I love her still;
   And whilst that virtue warms my heart,
   I'll love my handsome Nell.

Some beautiful girls I have seen,
   And many just as beautiful;
   But, for a modest graceful look,
   The like I never saw.

A beautiful girl, I will confess,

Is pleasant to the eye;
But, without some better qualities,
She's no a girl for me.

But Nelly's looks are gentle and sweet,
   And what is best of all;
   Her reputation is complete,
   And fair without a flaw.

She dresses always so clean and neat,
   Both decent and refined;
   And there's something in the way she walks
   Makes any dress look kind.

A showy dress and easy air,
   May slightly touch the heart;
   But it's innocence and modesty
   That polishes the dart.

It's this in Nelly that pleases me,
   It's this that enchants my soul;
   For absolutely in my heart
   She reigns without control.

A Little Extra...

We may never know exactly what inspired Robert to pick up the quill and paper and start to write, other than his obvious infatuation with Nelly. But, there is a story, that he heard Nelly sing a song written by the laird's son, (who was courting her at the time), and believed he could do better. Nelly is said to have loved singing songs when working - and had a sweet voice.

Years later Burns wrote about this song, saying:
"I never had the least thought or inclination of turning poet till I got once heartily in love, and then rhyme and song were, in a manner, the spontaneous language of my heart. I remember I composed it in a wild enthusiasm of passion and to this hour I never recollect it but my heart melts, and my blood sallies at the remembrance."

Nelly later married William Bone, a coachman to the laird of Newark.

Nelly Kilpatrick is also said to be the "Nell" mentioned in the poem "Halloween".

2
THE LASS O' CESSNOCK BANKS

This poem was written by Robert in 1780. At this point in time he was 22 years of age and working at Lochlea farm alongside his family. He was just beginning his journey as a poet and hadn't yet seen much life outside of farming. He had however, seen a girl walking by the banks of the river Cessnock and composed this poem / song for her.

Who Was The Lass O' Cessnock Banks ..?

Alison Begbie was the daughter of a poor farmer and is believed to have been born in the parish of Galston. At the time Robert knew her, she was working as a domestic servant in a house near the river Cessnock. This is where he first saw her, walking by the riverbanks.

Robert sent five letters to Alison, hoping to court her. In the first letter Robert writes that he hopes the recipient will not despise him because he is *"ignorant of the flattering arts of courtship"*. The fourth letter includes a proposal of marriage, *" If you will be so good and so generous as to admit me for your partner, your companion, your bosom friend through life, there is nothing on this side of eternity shall give me greater transport"*. It is thought that the fifth letter is an acknowledgment of refusal.

The Lass O' Cessnock Banks
By Robert Burns
Written: 1780
Type: Song / Poem

Tune: If he be a Butcher neat & trim

On Cessnock banks a lassie dwells;
    Could I describe her shape and mein;
    Our lasses a' she far excels,
    An' she has twa sparkling roguish een.

She's sweeter than the morning dawn,
    When rising Phoebus first is seen,
    And dew-drops twinkle o'er the lawn;
    An' she has twa, sparkling, roguish een.

She's stately, like yon youthful ash,
    That grows the cowslip braes between,
    And drinks the stream, with vigour fresh;
    An' she has twa, sparkling, roguish een.

She's spotless, like the flow'ring thorn.
    With flow'rs so white and leaves so green,
    When purest in the dewy morn;
    An' she has twa, sparkling, roguish een.

Her looks are like the vernal May,
    When ev'ning Phoebus shine's serene,
    While birds rejoice on every spray;
    An' she has twa, sparkling, roguish een.

Her hair is like the curling mist,
    That climbs the mountain-sides at e'en,
    When flow'r-reviving rains are past;
    And she has two sparkling roguish een.

Her forehead's like the show'ry bow,
    When gleaming sunbeams intervene,

  And gild the distant mountain's brow;
  And she has twa, sparkling, roguish een.

Her cheeks are like yon crimson gem,
  The pride of all the flowery scene,
  Just opening on its thorny stem;
  And she has twa, sparkling, roguish een.

Her bosom's like the nightly snow,
  When pale the morning rises keen,
  While hid the murm'ring streamlets flow;
  And she has twa, sparkling, roguish een.

Her lips are like yon cherries ripe,
  That sunny walls from Boreas screen;
  They tempt the taste and charm the sight;
  And she has twa, sparkling, roguish een.

Her teeth are like a flock of sheep,
  With fleeces newly washen clean,
  That slowly mount the rising steep;
  And she has twa, sparkling, roguish een.

Her breath, like the fragrant breeze,
> That gently stirs the blossom'd bean,
> When Phoebus sinks behind the seas;
> And she has twa, sparkling, roguish een.

Her voice is like the ev'ning thrush,
> That sings on Cessnock banks unseen,
> While his mate sits nestling in the bush;
> And she has twa, sparkling, roguish een.

But it's not her air, her form, her face.
> Tho' matching beauty's fabled queen;
> 'Tis the mind that shines in ev'ry grace,
> And chiefly in her roguish een.

The Lass O' Cessnock Banks
Translation

On Cessnock banks a girl dwells;
> *Could I describe her shape and form;*
> *All our girls she far excels,*
> *And she has two, sparkling, roguish eyes.*

She's sweeter than the morning dawn,
  When the rising sun first is seen,
  And dew-drops twinkle over the lawn;
  And she has two, Sparkling, roguish eyes.

She's stately, like yonder youthful ash,
  That grows the flowers on hills between,
  And drinks the stream with vigour fresh;
  And she has two, sparkling, roguish eyes.

She's spotless, like the flowering thorn.
  With flowers so white and leaves so green,
  When purest in the dewy morning;
  And she has two, sparkling, roguish eyes.

Her looks are like springtime in May,
  When evening sun shine's serene,
  While birds rejoice on every spray;
  And she has two, sparkling, roguish eyes.

Her hair is like the curling mist,
  That climbs the mountain-sides at evening,
  When flower-reviving rains are past;
  And she has two, sparkling, roguish eyes.

Her forehead's like the showery bow,
  When gleaming sunbeams intervene,
  And gild the distant mountain's brow;
  And she has two, sparkling, roguish eyes.

Her cheeks are like yonder crimson gem,
  The pride of all the flowery scene,
  Just opening on its thorny stem;
  And she has two, sparkling, roguish eyes.

Her bosom's like the nightly snow,
  When pale, the morning eagerly rises,
  While hid the murmering steamlets flow;
  And she has two, sparkling, roguish eyes.

Her lips are like yonder cherries ripe,
  That sunny walls from the wind screen;
  They tempt the taste and charm the sight;
  And she has two, sparkling, roguish eyes.

Her teeth are like a flock of sheep,
  With fleeces newly washed clean,

That slowly mount the rising steep;
And she has two, sparkling, roguish eyes.

Her breath like the fragrant breeze,
  That gently stirs the blossomd bean,
  When the sun sinks behind the seas;
  And she has two, sparkling, roguish eyes.

Her voice is like the evening thrush,
  That sings on Cessnock banks unseen,
  While his mate sits nestling in the bush;
  And she has two, sparkling, roguish eyes.

But it's not her air, her form, her face.
  Although matching beauty's fabled queen;
  It's the mind that shines in every grace,
  And chiefly in her roguish eyes.

A Little Extra…

It is believed that a few years after Alison turned down Roberts marriage proposal she moved to Glasgow. She met her future husband there, they married and settled down together.

This song was printed in *"Scots Musical Museum"*.

3
RIGS O' BARLEY

Robert wrote this song in 1782 whilst working on his fathers rented farm, "Lochlea" - which is near the town of Tarbolton. He was 24 years of age and had now clearly lost his boyhood innocence. This song shows his passion for women, a passion that follows him throughout his adult life.

The song itself is a simple tale of a romance during a meeting between Robert and Annie in the barley fields, (possibly the fields at Lochlea or Adamhill ?). They met, they walked through the fields, spent a few intimate hours together and then parted. It is obvious from the last verse that Robert thought this was a very special night indeed and treasures the memory of it.

"Rigs" are the ridges and furrows in a field. They are created when a field has been ploughed.

Who was Annie..?

Although Burns himself never confirmed who Annie was, there is a lot of speculation that it was Anne Rankie. Anne was the daughter of John Rankie, the tenant farmer at Adamhill farm, which was just two miles from Lochlea. John was a friend of Roberts and was once described by him as *"rough, rude, ready witted Rankie"*. Robert knew Anne well and was said to have been *"passionately fond of her"*. Robert is known to have given her a gift of a locket of his hair and a miniature painting of himself - which she treasured all of her life.

Rigs O' Barley
    By Robert Burns
    Written: 1782
    Type: Song
    Tune: Corn Rigs are Bonnie

It was upon a Lammas night,
    When corn rigs are bonie,
    Beneath the moon's unclouded light,
    I held awa to Annie;
    The time flew by, wi' tentless heed,
    Till, 'tween the late and early,
    Wi' sma' persuasion she agreed

To see me thro' the barley.

Corn rigs, an' barley rigs,
    An' corn rigs are bonie;
    I'll ne'er forget that happy night,
    Amang the rigs wi' Annie.

The sky was blue, the wind was still,
    The moon was shining clearly;
    I set her down, wi' right good will,
    Amang the rigs o' barley:
    I ken't her heart was a' my ain;
    I lov'd her most sincerely;
    I kiss'd her owre and owre again,
    Amang the rigs o' barley.

Corn rigs, an' barley rigs,
    An' corn rigs are bonie;
    I'll ne'er forget that happy night,
    Amang the rigs wi' Annie.

I lock'd her in my fond embrace;
    Her heart was beating rarely:
    My blessings on that happy place,

Amang the rigs o' barley!
But by the moon and stars so bright,
That shone that hour so clearly!
She aye shall bless that happy night,
Amang the rigs o' barley.

Corn rigs, an' barley rigs,
   An' corn rigs are bonie;
   I'll ne'er forget that happy night,
   Amang the rigs wi' Annie.

I hae been blythe wi comrades dear;
   I hae been merry drinking;
   I hae been joyfu' gath'rin gear;
   I hae been happy thinking:
   But a' the pleasures e'er I saw,
   Tho' three times doubl'd fairly,
   That happy night was worth them a'
   Amang the rigs o' barley.

Rigs O' Barley
   Translation

It was upon the night of August 1st,

When corn rigs are so pretty,
Beneath the moon's unclouded light,
I went to meet with Annie;
The time flew by without a care,
Until between the late and early,
With little persuasion she agreed
To see me through the barley.

Corn rigs and barley rigs,
    And corn rigs are pretty;
    I'll never forget that happy night,
    Among the rigs with Annie.

The sky was blue, the wind was still,
    The moon was shining clearly;
I sat her down, with right good will,
    Among the rigs o' barley:
I knew her heart was all my own;
I loved her most sincerely;
I kissed her over and over again,
    Among the rigs o' barley.

Corn rigs and barley rigs,
    And corn rigs are pretty;
    I'll never forget that happy night,

Among the rigs with Annie.

I locked her in my fond embrace;
    Her heart was beating quickly:
    My blessings on that happy place,
    Among the rigs o' barley!
    But by the moon and stars so bright,
    That shone that hour so clearly!
    She'll always bless that happy night,
    Among the rigs o' barley.

Corn rigs and barley rigs,
    And corn rigs are pretty;
    I'll never forget that happy night,
    Among the rigs with Annie.

I've been happy with friends dear;
    I've been merry drinking;
    I've been joyful gathering possessions;
    I've been happy thinking:
    But all the pleasures ever I saw,
    Although three times doubled fairly,
    That happy night was worth them all
    Among the rigs of barley.

A little extra …

Anne married an inn-keeper called John Merry, who died in 1802. She ran the inn herself until 1843, eventually retiring at the age of 84. Robert is known to have stayed at the inn in August 1786, four years after the song was written.

4
THE LASS O' BALLOCHMYLE

This poem was written in 1786. The first verse sets the scene of Robert out for a walk enjoying all the splendour nature has to offer, dewy fields, birds singing, etc. The second verse see him chance upon a beautiful girl. In verse three he describes her beauty and in verse four wishes they were social equals so that he could woe her. In the final verse he says that he would not want seek his fortune on the seas or dig for gold but would want nothing more than work a farm to support and love the bonnie lass o' Ballochmyle.

Who was 'The Lass o' Ballochmyle"..?

The Ballochmyle estate was close to Mossgiel farm and Robert could easily have wandered onto its lands and seen **Wilhemina Alexander**, (The Lass o' Ballochmyle), out walking. The estate was very rich and the people that owned it, Claud Alexander and his sister Wilhemina, were on a much higher social standing than Robert's family.

Robert wrote to Wilhemina and enclosed the song, asking her permission to publish it in his second book of poems, (this may have been a way of ingratiating himself with the Alexander family). At the time Wilhelmina was 30 years old and quiet plain looking, she therefore thought Robert was teasing her and never replied to him.

The Lass O' Ballochmyle
By Robert Burns
Written: 1786
Type: Poem /Song
Tune: Ettrick Banks

'Twas even, the dewy fields were green,
On every blade the pearls hang;
The zephyr wanton'd round the bean,
And bore its fragrant sweets alang:
In every glen the mavis sang,
All nature list'ning seem'd the while,
Except where greenwood echoes rang,
Amang the braes o' Ballochmyle.

With careless step I onward stray'd,

My heart rejoic'd in nature's joy,
When, musing in a lonely glade,
A maiden fair I chanc'd to spy:
Her air like nature's vernal smile:
Perfection whisper'd, passing by,
"Behold the lass o' Ballochmyle!"

Fair this morn in flowery May,
    And sweet is night in autumn mild,
    When roving thro' the garden gay,
    Or wand'ring in the lonely wild:
    But woman, nature's darling child!
    There all her charms she does compile;
    Even there her other works are foil'd
    By the bonie lass o' Ballochmyle.

O' had she been a country maid,
    And I the happy country swain,
    Tho' shelter'd in the lowest shed
    That ever rose on Scotland's plain!
    Thro' weary winter's wind and rain,
    With joy, with rapture, I would toil;
    And nightly to my bosom strain
    The Bonie lass o' Ballochmyle.

Then pride might climb the slipp'ry steep,
    Where frame and honours lofty shine;
    And thirst of gold might tempt the deep,
    Or downward seek the Indian mine:
    Give me the cot below the pine,
    To tend the flocks or till the soil;
    And ev'ry day have joys divine
    With the bonie lass o' Ballochmyle

The Lass O' Ballochmyle
Translation

It was evening, the dewy fields were green,
    On every blade the pearls hang;
    The zephyr wandered round the bean,
    And bore its fragrant sweets along:
    In every glen the thrush sang,
    All nature listening seemed the while,
    Except where greenwood echoes rang,
    Among the hills of Ballochmyle.

With careless step I onward strayed,
    My heart rejoiced in nature's joy,
    When, thinking in a lonely glade,
    A maiden fair I chanced to spy:

Her air like nature's youthful smile:
Perfection whispered, passing by,
"Behold the girl of Ballochmyle!"

Fair this morning in flowery May,
And sweet is night in autumn mild,
When walking through the garden gay,
Or wandering in the lonely wild:
But woman, nature's darling child!
There all her charms she does compile;
Even there her other works are foiled
By the beautiful girl of Ballochmyle.

Oh had she been a country maid,
And I the happy country suitor,
Although sheltered in the lowest shed
That ever rose on Scotland's plain!
Through weary winter's wind and rain,
With joy, with rapture, I would toil;
And nightly to my bosom pull
The beautiful girl of Ballochmyle.

Then pride might climb the slippery slope,
Where frame and honours lofty shine;
And thirst of gold might tempt the deep,

Or downward seek the Indian mine:
Give me the cot below the pine,
To tend the flocks or till the soil;
And every day have joys divine
With the beautiful girl of Ballochmyle

A Little Extra…

Wihelmina never married and when she died, (at the age of 87), this song was one of her most precious possessions.

1786 was a significant year for Robert. He was, at that time, single and living with his family at Mossgiel farm. His first published work, "Poems chiefly in the Scottish dialect", known as "The Kilmarnock Edition", was published and sold out within one month. He became the father of twins, (Robert and Jean), by Jean Armour, (he was already the father of one illegitimate child, (Elizabeth), by Elizabeth Paton – his mothers servant).

He abandoned his plans to emigrate to Jamaica. This was probably due to the death of Mary Campbell, (Highland Mary), and then travelled to Edinburgh seeking to publish his second edition of poems.

5
TO MARY IN HEAVEN

This poem was written by Robert in 1789, on the third anniversary of Highland Mary's death. A few years after Robert's death, his wife Jean was asked about the day this poem was written. She tells us this:

"He grew sad about something, went into the barnyard, where he strode restlessly up and down for sometime, although repeatedly asked to come in. Immediately on entering the house he sat down and wrote, To Mary in Heaven."

Who was Highland Mary ?

Mary Campbell was the daughter of Archibald and Agnes Campbell of Auchamore, which is near Dunoon on the Firth of Clyde. Archibald was a seaman and Mary was the eldest of his four childen. Mary also lived with her family in Campeltown, (this is probably why she has the nickname "Highland Mary"), and Greenock. She then moved to Ayrshire and started work in Gavin Hamilton's house as a domestic servant. Gavin Hamilton was a good friend of Robert's and it is likely this is where they first met.

Mary was the woman Robert turned to, (in 1786), when he was not allowed to marry Jean Armour. Reports as to Mary's character are varied, but many of Robert's friends tried to persuade him to end the relationship, as they believed she was not good enough for him. Despite this advice, Robert and Mary exchanged Bibles in a rustic marriage ceremony and prepared to live together, possibly moving to Jamaica.

To Mary in Heaven
By Robert Burns
Written: 1789
Type: Poem

Thou ling'ring star with less'ning ray,
    That lov'st to greet the early morn,
    Again thou usher'st in the day
    My Mary from my soul was torn.
    O Mary! dear departed shade !
    Where is thy place of blissful rest?
    See'st thou thy lover lowly laid?

    Hear'st thou the groans that rend his breast?

That sacred hour can I forget?
    Can I forget the hallowed grove,
    Where by the winding Ayr we met,
    To live one day of parting love?
    Eternity will not efface
    Those records dear of transports past;
    Thy image at our last embrace;
    Ah! little thought we't was our last!

Ayr, gurgling, kiss'd his pebbled shore,
    O'erhung with wild woods thick'ning green;
    The fragrant birch and hawthorn hoar,
    Twin'd am'rous round the raptur'd scene:
    The flow'rs sprang wanton to be prest,
    The birds sang love on every spray,
    Till too, too soon, the glowing west,
    Proclaim'd the speed of winged day.

Still o'er these scenes my mem'ry wakes,
    And fondly broods with miser care!
    Time but th' impression stronger makes,
    As streams their channels deeper wear.
    My Mary! Dear departed shade!

Where is thy place of blissful rest?
See'st thou thy lover lowly laid?
Hear'st thou the groans that rend his breast?

To Mary in Heaven
Translation

Your lingering star with lessening ray,
    That loves to greet the early morning,
    Again you usher in the day
    My Mary from my soul was torn.
    O Mary! Dear departed shade!
    Where is your place of blissful rest?
    Do you see your lover lowly laid?
    Do you hear the groans that split his breast?

That sacred hour can I forget?
    Can I forget the hallowed grove,
    Where by the winding Ayr we met,
    To live one day of parting love?
    Eternity will not erase
    Those records dear of transports past;
    Your image at our last embrace;
    Ah! little thought it was our last!

Ayr, gurgling kissed his pebbled shore,
 Overhung with wild woods thickening green;
 The fragrant birch and hawthorn frost,
 Twined amorous round the raptured scene:
 The flowers sprang resisting being pressed,
 The birds sang love on every spray,
 Till too, too soon, the glowing west,
 Proclaimed the speed of winged day.

Still over these scenes my memory wakes,
 And fondly broods with miser care!
 Time but the impression stronger makes,
 As streams their channels deeper wear.
 My Mary! Dear departed shade!
 Where is your place of blissful rest?
 Do you see your lover lowly laid?
 Do you hear the groans that split his breast?

A Little Extra ...

Unfortunately, soon after exchanging bibles with Robert, Mary died of a fever in Greenock. When Robert heard of Mary's death, he abandoned his plans to relocate to Jamaica.

Mrs Todd, (Gavin Hamilton's married daughter), remembered Mary being in their house in 1785 to look after her brother, Alexander. She described Mary as "pleasant and winning, though not a beauty", she also said Mary was "tall fair haired with blue eyes".

Robert also wrote these poems about Mary:
    Highland Mary
    The Highland lassie
    Will ye go to the Indies, my Mary
    Burn's lament to Mary

6
AE FOND KISS

This is one of Roberts best known love poems / songs. It is sung and recited at lots of Burns nights, music festivals, parties and get-togethers.

Robert wrote 'Ae Fond Kiss' in 1791 when he was forced to part ways with a woman called 'Nancy'. Their relationship, (which had lasted for several years), ended when Nancy sailed to Jamaica to try to reconcile with her husband.

Who was Nancy ?

Agnes Craig, known as 'Nancy' to her friends, was an educated and attractive woman. She was the daughter of a Glasgow surgeon, Andrew Craig, but was also descended from a long line of ministers and was raised with a strong moral code. She had married at the age of seventeen, (against the wishes of her family), to James M'lehose and had four children with him in four years. Nancy left her husband due to his cruelty towards her.

Nancy met Robert at a tea party in Edinburgh on the 4th December 1787. There was an immediate attraction and they arranged another meeting. They met and corresponded for several years. They wrote to each other under the false names 'Clarinda' and 'Sylvander,' they did this because the correspondence was rather passionate and they did not want their true identities to be discovered. Robert longed for a physical relationship with Nancy but this was not to be. In one of Nancy's letters she included this verse:

Talk not of love, it gives me pain,
    For love has been my foe;
    He bound me with an iron chain,
    And plunged me deep in woe…
    Your friendship much can make me blest,
    O, why that bliss destroy!
    Why urge the odious, one request
    You know I must deny!

Ae Fond Kiss
    By Robert Burns
    Written: 1791
    Type: Poem /Song

Ae fond kiss, and then we sever;
    Ae fareweel, alas for ever!
    Deep in heart-wrung tears I'll pledge thee,
    Warring sighs and groans I'll wage thee.

Who shall say that fortune grieves him,
    While the star of hope she leaves him?
    Me, nae cheerful twinkle lights me;
    Dark despair around benights me.

I'll ne'er blame my partial fancy,
    Naething could resist my Nancy:
    But to see her was to love her;
    Love but her, and love forever.

Had we never lov'd sae kindly,
    Had we never lov'd sae blindly,
    Never met, or never parted,
    We had ne'er been broken-hearted.

Fare-thee-weel thou first and fairest!
    Fare-thee-weel thou best and dearest!

Thine be ilka joy and treasure,
Peace, enjoyment, love and pleasure!

Ae fond kiss, and then we sever!
    Ae fareweel, alas for ever!
    Deep in heart-wrung tears I'll pledge thee,
    Warring sighs and groans I'll wage thee.

Ae Fond Kiss
    Translation

One fond kiss, and then we sever!
    One farewell, alas forever!
    Deep in heart-wrung tears I'll pledge you,
    Warring sighs and groans I'll wage you.

Who shall say that fortune grieves him,
    While the star of hope she leaves him?
    Me, no cheerful twinkle lights me;
    Dark despair around overtakes me.

I'll never blame my partial fancy,
    Nothing could resist my Nancy:

But to see her was to love her;
Love but her, and love forever.

Had we never loved so kindly,
    Had we never loved so blindly,
    Never met, or never parted,
    We had never been broken-hearted.

Fare-you-well you first and fairest!
    Fare-you-well you best and dearest!
    Yours be every joy and treasure,
    Peace, enjoyment, love and pleasure!

One fond kiss, and then we sever!
    One farewell, alas forever!
    Deep in heart-wrung tears I'll pledge you,
    Warring sighs and groans I'll wage you.

A little extra…

When Nancy arrived in Jamaica to reconcile with her husband, James M'lehose, she found he had taken up with a Negro slave and they had a daughter together. She returned home, taking passage on the return voyage of the ship she arrived in. When she arrived home she found that Robert's passion for her had cooled.

At the same time as his plutonic relationship with Nancy, Robert had a physical relationship with her domestic servant, Jenny Clow. Jenny was occasionally sent to deliver the letters between Nancy, (Clarinda), and Robert, (Sylvander). In 1788 Jenny became pregnant and had a son, 'Robert Burns Clow.' Unfortunately Jenny died of tuberculosis in 1792, at the tender age of 24. However, her son had a happier life, he eventually moved to England and became a wealthy merchant. His son, (Robert's grandson), also called Robert Burns Clow, was a trader in the East Indies until he was killed by pirates in September 1851.

Robert also wrote these poems about Nancy:
    Answer to Clarinda
    Sylvander to Clarinda
    Revision for Clarinda
    Clarinda, Mistress of my soul
    To Clarinda – (with a present of a pair of wine glasses)
    Gloomy December

Behold the hour, the boat arrive

7
I LOVE MY JEAN

This was written by Robert in 1788 during a brief period of separation from his wife. They were still in their honeymoon period but Robert was at Ellisland, preparing a home for them, while Jean stayed at Mossgiel.

Who was Jean ..?

Jean Armour was born in Mauchline in 1765 and was the second oldest of eleven children. Her father was James Armour, a stonemason, and her mother was Mary Smith Armour. It is said that she first met Robert around 1784 on a drying green when she chased his dog away from her laundry. After Robert wrote about some of the girls in the neighborhood she became known as one of the "Belles o' Mauchline". Eventually, after a few proposals and four children together, she became Robert's wife.

Robert and Jean had a relationship in 1786, which ended up with Jean giving birth to twins. Robert tried to marry Jean when he found out that she was pregnant, but her parents would not allow it and sent her to a different part of the country to live with an aunt. When Robert returned from Edinburgh in 1787 he was treated as a celebrity and the Armour family were now in favor of marriage. Even at this point in time things didn't run smoothly between the pair, as Jean became pregnant again and was thrown out of her family home. Robert took Jean in and they were married on August 5th, 1788.

It is difficult to describe the marriage between Robert and Jean as it had many ups and downs. Robert was affectionate towards Jean but there is little evidence of love or passion, there are only four recorded letters from Robert to Jean - compared with the 60, (ish), letters he wrote to Nancy McLehose. There are also only five or possibly six poems, which Robert wrote directly about Jean.

I Love My Jean
    By Robert Burns
    Written: 1788
    Type: Song / Poem
    Tune: Miss Admiral Gordon's Strathspey

Of a' the airts the wind can blaw,
    I dearly like the West;
    For there the bony lassie lives,
    The lassie I lo'e best:
    There's wild-woods grow and rivers row,
    And mony a hill between:
    But day and night my fancies flight,
    Is ever wi' my Jean.

I see her in the dewy flowers,
    I see her sweet and fair;
    I hear her in the tunefu' birds,
    I hear her charm the air:
    There's not a bony flower that springs,
    By fountain, shaw, or green;
    There's not a bony bird that sings,
    But minds me o' my Jean.

I Love My Jean
    Translation

Of all the directions the wind can blow,
    I dearly like the west;

For there the beautiful girl lives,
The girl I love the best:
There's wild-woods grow and rivers flow,
And many a hill between:
But day and night my fancies flight,
Is ever with my Jean.

I see her in the dewy flowers,
I see her sweet and fair;
I hear her in the tuneful birds,
I hear her charm the air:
There's not a beautiful flower that springs,
By fountain, woods, or green;
There's not a beautiful bird that sings,
But reminds me of my Jean.

A Little Extra ……
Robert and Jean had nine children together, (their last child was born on the day of Robert's funeral).

She outlived him by 38 years.

Robert also wrote these poems about Jean:
    O' were I on Parnassus hill
    The Northern lass
    It is na, Jean, thy bonie face

O, wat ye wha's in yon town
The groves o' sweet myrtle

8
BEWARE O' BONIE ANN

This poem was written in 1789. At this time Robert was just beginning to work as an excise officer and was living at Ellisland, near Dumfries. In this year Robert became a father again, as Jean gave birth to "Francis Wallace Burns".

Who was Ann ..?

Ann Masterton was the daughter of Allan Masterton, a school teacher and good friend of Robert's. Robert wrote the song as a compliment to Ann and probably as a favor to his friend, Allan Masterton.

Beware O' Bonnie Ann
By Robert Burns
    Written: 1789
    Type: Song / Poem

Ye gallants bright I rede you right,
    Beware o' bonie Ann;

Her comely face sae fu' o' grace,
Your heart she will trepan:
Her een sae bright like stars by night,
Her skin sae like the swan;
Sae jimply lac'd her genty waist,
That sweetly ye may span.

Youth, Grace, and Love attendant move,
And pleasure leads the van:
In A' their charms and conquering arms,
They wait on Bonie Ann.
The captive bands may chain the hands,
But love enslaves the man:
Ye gallants braw, I rede you a',
Beware o' bonie Ann !

Beware O' Bonnie Ann
Translation

You worthy men, I advise you truthfully,
Beware of Beautiful Ann;
Her pleasing face so full of grace,
Your heart she will ensnare:
Her eye's so bright like stars by night,
Her skin so like the swan;

So neatly corseted, her slender waist,
That sweetly you may span.

Youth, Grace, and Love attendant move,
And pleasure leads the group:
In all their charms and conquering arms,
They wait on beautiful Ann.
The captive bands may chain the hands,
But love enslaves the man:
You worthy, handsome men, I advise you all,
Beware of beautiful Ann !

A Little extra …

Ann married a Dr. Derbyshire, they had one son together and lived in Bath and London.

9
THE GOWDEN LOCKS OF ANNA

At the time of writing this poem Robert is 30 years of age, married to Jean Armour and living at Ellisland farm near Dumfries.

Robert's love of women is again clearly showing through in this poem. At first glance you might think that this is another poem by Robert, which is intended to flatter a women he has an interest in. Unfortunately this describes an affair he had with Anna. He tells us of the time he spent with Anna and the huge amount this meant to him.

Who was Anna ..?

Helen Anne Park, (known as 'Anna'), was the niece of a Mrs Hyslop, who ran the "Globe Tavern," in Dumfries. Anna worked in the tavern alongside her aunt. There is very little known of her relationship with Robert except that it brought about another illegitimate child - 'Elizabeth'.

Not much is known about what happen to Anna after her relationship with Robert. J DeLancey Ferguson, (a well respected Burns Scholar), believes she died giving birth to Elizabeth. Another story alleges she became a domestic servant in Leith / Edinburgh, married a soldier and died giving birth to his child.

The Gowden Locks of Anna
By Robert Burns
  Written: 1790
  Type: Poem/ Song

Yestreen, I had a pint o' wine,
  A place where body saw na;
  Yestereen lay on this breast o' mine
  The Gowden locks of Anna.

The hungry Jew in wilderness,
  Rejoicing o'er his manna,
  Was naething to my hinny bliss
  Upon the lips of Anna.

Ye monarchs, take the east and west
  Frae Indus to Savannah;

Gie me, within my straining grasp,
    The melting form of Anna.

There I'll despise Imperial charms,
    An Empress or Sultana,
    While dying raptures in her arms
    I give and take wi' Anna!

Awa, thou flaunting God of day!
    Awa, thou pale Diana!
    Ilk star, gae hide thy twinkling ray,
    When I'm to meet my Anna!

Come, in thy raven plumage, night,
    Sun, Moon and Stars, withdrawn a';
    And bring an angel-pen to write
    My transports with my Anna!

The Kirk and State may join an' tell,
    To do sic things I maunna:
    The Kirk and State may gae to hell,
    And I'll gae to my Anna.

She is the sunshine o' my e'e,
    To live but her I canna;
    Had I on earth but wishes three,
    The first would be my Anna.

The Gowden Locks of Anna
    Translation

Last night I had a pint of wine,
    In a place where nobody saw;
    Last night lay on this breast of mine
    The Golden locks of Anna.

The hungry Jew in the wilderness,
    Rejoicing over his manna,
    Was nothing to my honey bliss,
    Upon the lips of Anna.

You, kings take the east and west
    From Indus to Savannah;
    Give me within my straining grasp
    The melting form of Anna!

There I will despise imperial charms,
   An empress or Sultana,
   While dying raptures in her arms
   I give and take with Anna!

Away you flaunting God of day!
   Away, you pale Diana!
   Each star go hide your twinkling ray,
   When I'm to meet my Anna!

Come in, you raven plumage night,
   Sun, Moon and Stars, withdrawn all;
   And bring an Angel-pen to write,
   My transports with my Anna.

The Church and State may join, and tell,
   To do such things I must not:
   The Church and State may go to hell,
   And I will go to my Anna.

She is the sunshine of my eye,
   To live without her I cannot;
   Had I on earth but wishes three,
   The first would be my Anna.

A Little Extra…

Whatever happened to Anna, one thing is certain - Robert took the baby, (Elizabeth), and gave her to his wife, Jean Armour, to raise as one of their family. Jean agreed to do this even although at the time she was heavily pregnant. Jean gave birth to 'William Nicol Burns' nine days after taking in Elizabeth.

Manna- food from heaven
Indus – a river in southern Asia

10
THE BONNIE WEE THING

In 1791 Robert moved to Dumfries and was living with his wife and family. In that same year Robert and Jean had another son - William Nicol Burns. During this time he was working as an excise officer.

"The Bonie Wee Thing" was a poem written about a woman Robert wanted to be with. It needs little explanation as it clearly shows his feelings about her, indeed, it is meant to flatter her. In the poem Robert wants to be with her, but the closest he gets is merely to look upon her.

Who Was The Bonnie Wee Thing ..?

Deborah Duff Davies was the daughter of Dr Daniel Davies of Tenby in Pembrokeshire. Writing to Mrs Dunlop in June 1793 Robert described her as *"positively the least creature ever I saw, to be at the same time unexceptionably, and indeed uncommonly handsome and beautiful"*. Deborah was a friend of the Riddell family, (from Mauchline), Robert was also a friend of the Riddell's.

Deborah was in a much higher social circle than Robert, which meant she would have had little to do with him.

The Bonnie Wee Thing
By Robert Burns
    Written: 1791
    Type: Poem / Song

Bonie wee thing, cannie wee thing,
    Lovely wee thing, wert thou mine,
    I wad wear thee in my bosom,
    Lest my jewel I should tine.

Wishfully I look and languish
    In that bonie face o' thine,
    And my heart it stounds wi' anguish,
    Lest my wee thing be na mine.

Bonie wee thing, cannie wee thing,

Lovely wee thing, wert thou mine,
I wad wear thee in my bosom,
Lest my jewel I should tine.

Wit, and grace, and Love, and Beauty,
    In ae constellation shine;
    To adore thee is my duty,
    Goddess o' this soul o' mine!

Bonie wee thing, cannie wee thing,
    Lovely wee thing, wert thou mine,
    I wad wear thee in my bosom,
    Lest my jewel I should tine.

The Bonnie Wee Thing
Translation

Pretty wee thing, gentle wee thing,
    Lovely wee thing, if you were mine,
    I would wear you in my bosom,
    In case my jewel I should lose.

Wishfully I look and languish

At that pretty face of yours,
And my heart, it aches with torment,
In case my wee thing is not mine.

Pretty wee thing, gentle wee thing,
   Lovely wee thing, if you were mine,
   I would wear you in my bosom,
   In case my jewel I should lose.

Wit, and Grace, and Love, and Beauty,
   In one constellation shine;
   To adore you is my duty,
   Goddess of this soul of mine!

Pretty wee thing, gentle wee thing,
   Lovely wee thing, if you were mine,
   I would wear you in my bosom,
   In case my jewel I should lose.

A Little Extra...

Deborah went abroad in an attempt to improve her health but unfortunately died young of consumption, (now known as tuberculosis).

Robert also wrote these poems about Deborah:
  Lovely Davis
  Epigram on Miss Davis

In this year, (1791), Robert also had a daughter, (Elizabeth), with Ann Park. Ann was a barmaid at the "Globe Tavern" in Dumfries.

11
THE RIGHTS OF A WOMAN

This address was written for a very specific purpose, it was to be read out at a benefit night held at the Dumfries Theatre on the 26th November 1792. It would have shocked audiences, as it is reminiscent of, "the rights of a man", by Thomas Paine, but soon goes on to talk of the Rights of women - a highly unpopular topic in Burn's lifetime.

Who inspired this poem ?

Louisa Fontenelle, born 1773. Louisa was a touring actress based in London. She first appeared on stage at Covent Garden on the 6th November 1788 playing the role of "Molly" in the play, "The Highland Reel", by O'Keefe. It is likely that Louisa toured the country with the same production as she played the same role at Edinburgh's Theatre Royal on the 17th October 1789.

Robert saw her when she performed at the Dumfries theatre in 1792. He wrote to her soon after seeing her and offered the address to her to be used at her benefit night. In the same letter he also said:

"To you madam, on our humble Dumfries boards, I have been more indebted for entertainment, than ever I was in prouder theatres. Your charms as a woman would ensure applause to the most indifferent actress, and your theatrical talents would secure the admiration to the plainest figure."

Robert wrote this poem about Louisa, "on seeing her in a favorite character":

Sweet naivete of feature,
    Simple, wild, enchanting elf,
    Not to thee, but thanks to nature,
    Thou art acting but thyself.
    Wert thou awkward, stiff, affected,
    Spurning nature, torturing art;
    Loves and gracies all rejected,
    then indeed thou'dst act a part.

The Rights of a Woman
By: Robert Burns
Written: 1792
Type: Address

While Europe's eye is fix'd on mighty things,
    The fate of Empires and the fall of Kings;
    While quacks of State must each produce his plan,
    And even children lisp the Rights of Man;
    Amid this mighty fuss just let me mention,
    The Rights of Woman merit some attention.

First, in the Sexes' intermix'd connection,
    One sacred Right of Woman is protection.
    The tender flower that lifts its head, elate,
    Helpless, must fall before the blasts of Fate,
    Sunk on earth defac'd its lovely form,
    Unless your shelter ward th' impending storm.

Our second Right but needless here is caution,
    To keep that right inviolate's the fashion;
    Each man of sense has it so full before him,
    He'd die before he'd wrong it 'tis decorum.
    There was, indeed in far less polish'd days,
    A time, when rough rude man had naughty ways,

Would swagger, swear, get drunk, kick up a riot,
Nay even thus invade a Lady's quiet.

Now, thank our stars! those Gothic times are fled;
    Now, well bred men and you are all well–bred,
    Most justly think and we are much the gainers,
    Such conduct neither spirit, wit, or manners.

For right the third, our last our best, our dearest,
    That right to female fluttering hearts the nearest;
    Which even the rights of Kings in low prostration,
    Most humbly own-'tis dear dear admiration!
    In that blest sphere alone we live and move;
    There taste that life of life immortal love.
    Smiles, glances, sighs tears, fits, flirtation, airs;
    'Gainst such an host what flinty savage dares,
    When awful Beauty joins with all her charms,
    Who is so rash as rise in rebel arms?

But truce with Kings and truce with constitutions,
    With bloody armaments and revolutions;
    Let Majesty your first attention summon,
    Ah! ca ira!
    The Majesty of a Woman!

The Rights of a Woman
  Translation

While Europe's eye is fixed on mighty things,
  The fate of Empires and the fall of Kings;
  While quacks of State must each produce his plan,
  And even children lisp the Rights of Man;
  Amid this mighty fuss let me just mention,
  The Rights of Woman merit some attention.

First in the sexes intermixed connection,
  One sacred right of Woman is protection.
  The tender flower that lifts its head, elate,
  Helpless must fall before the blasts of Fate,
  Sunk on earth defaced its lovely form,
  Unless your shelter protects from the impending storm.

Our second Right but heedless here is caution,
  To keep that Right untouched is the fashion;
  Each man of sense has it so full before him,
  He'd die before he'd wrong it it is decorum.
  There was indeed in far less polished days,
  A time when rough rude man had naughty ways,
  Would swagger, swear get drunk, kick up a riot,

No, even thus invade a lady's quiet.

Now, thank our stars! those Gothic times are fled;
    Now, well bred men and you are all well-bred,
    Most justly think and we are much the gainers,
    Such conduct neither spirit, wit, or manners.

For right the third, our last our best, our dearest,
    That right to female fluttering hearts the nearest;
    Which even the rights of Kings in low subservience,
    Most humbly own this dear dear admiration!
    In that blessed sphere alone we live and move;
    There taste that life of life immortal love.
    Smiles, glances, sighs tears, fits, flirtation, airs;
    Against such a host what hard savage dares,
    When awful Beauty joins with all her charms,
    Who is so rash as rise in rebel arms?

But truce with Kings and truce with constitutions,
    With bloody armaments and revolutions;
    Let Majesty your first attention summon,
    Ah! let it be!
    The Majesty of a woman!

A little extra…

Louisa married John Brown Williamson, an actor and manager of the Dumfries Theatre. They immigrated to America and played to audiences in Boston, New York….

Unfortunately their happiness was short lived as Louisa died of yellow fever in Charleston on the 30th of October 1799. She was just 26 years old.

Robert also wrote a second address for Miss Fontenelle. This was to be read out at her benefit night on the 4th of December 1793, at the Dumfries Theatre. The first line of the address is: "Still anxious to secure your partial favour".

12
LOVELY YOUNG JESSIE

In 1793, the year he wrote 'Lovely Young Jessie', Robert lived in a house in Mill Vennel, (now called Burns Street), Dumfries with his wife and family. At this point in his life he was working as an excise officer, but was suffering from ill health.

Who was Jessie, (Jessy) ..?

Jessy Lewars was the youngest daughter of John Lewars, Supervisor of the excise at Dumfries. When Jessy's father passed away, she and her brother John, (A fellow excise officer), lived in the house opposite Robert's and Jean's house in Mill Vennel. They were well known, (and well liked), by both Robert and Jean.

Robert very probably met Jessy for the first time in Mill Vennel, Dumfries. It is also almost certain that Robert and Jessy never had a physical relationship. The poems that Robert wrote about her were much more likely to have been inspired by her youth and beauty. Robert merely imagined himself as her strong, young lover.

Lovely Young Jessie
By Robert Burns
    Written: 1793
    Type: Poem

True hearted was he, the sad swain o' the Yarrow,
    And fair are the maids on the banks of the Ayr;
    But by the sweet side o' the Nith's winding river,
    Are lovers as faithful and maidens as fair:
    To equal young Jessie seek Scotland all over;
    To equal young Jessie you seek it in vain,
    Grace, beauty and elegance fetter her lover,
    And maidenly modesty fixes the chain.

O' fresh is the rose in the gay, dewy morning,
    And sweet is the lily at evenings close;
    But in the fair presence o' lovely young Jessie,
    Unseen is the lily, unheeded the rose.
    Love sits in her smile, a wizard ensnaring;
    Enthron'd in her een he delivers his law:
    And still to her charms she alone is a stranger;

Her modest demeanor's the jewel of a'.

Lovely Young Jessie
Translation

True hearted was he, the sad lover of the flowers,
  And fair are the maids on the banks of the Ayr;
  But by the sweet side o' the Nith's winding river,
  Are lovers as faithful and maidens as fair:
  To equal young Jessie seek Scotland all over;
  To equal young Jessie you seek it in vain,
  Grace, beauty and elegance bind her lover,
  And maidenly modesty fixes the chain.

Oh fresh is the rose in the gay, dewy morning,
  And sweet is the lily at evenings close;
  But in the presence of lovely young Jessie,
  Unseen is the lily unheeded the rose.
  Love sits in her smile a wizard ensnaring;
  Enthroned in her eye he delivers his law:
  And still to her charms she alone is a stranger;
  Her modest demeanour's the jewel of all.

A Little Extra…

In the final six months of Robert's life Jessy helped Jean to nurse him. Jessy also helped look after Robert and Jean's children after his death. Robert's eldest son, (also called Robert), remained with her for a year.

In 1799 Jessy Lewars married James Thomson, (he was also a writer). Together they had five sons and two daughters. When Jessy died, she was buried in St Michael's Churchyard - quite close to Robert's grave.

Robert also wrote these poems about Jessy:
    Here's a health to ane I lo'e dear
    The Menagerie
    The Toast
    Jessy's Illness
    Her recovery
    Inscription – This is written on the copy of "The Scots Musical Museum", which he gave to Jessy. The inscription was dated 26th June 1796, Robert died on the 25th of July 1796.

As well as working full time, Robert continued to collect and write songs which were eventually published in "Scots Musical Museum" and "Select Scottish Airs". Two of these songs were *'Scots wha Hae'* and *'Auld Land Syne'*. He did this work because he felt it was important and he enjoyed it. Robert never expected, or received, any monetary payment for this.

GLOSSARY

One of the biggest barriers to understanding Burns poetry is the old and unusual Scottish dialect he often used. Although, to be fair, he was born over 250 years ago...

This glossary of Scottish words and there modern English translation should help you to break down the language barrier.

A
a' - all
albeit - although
abeigh - at a distance
aboon - above
abread - abrod, in sight
abreed - in breadth
a-bodie - someone
awbodie - everyone
acquent - acquainted
acqueesh - between
a'day - all day long
adle - putrid water
ado - to do
ae - one

aff - off
aff -loof - off hand
afiel - afield
afore - before
aften - often
agee - on the side
agley - wrong, askew
ahin - behind
aiblins - perhaps
aik - oak
aiker - acre
ail - ill
ain - own
air - early
airless - money
airn - iron, iron tool
airt - direction
aith - oath
aits - oats
aisle - hot cinder
akwart - awkward
alake - alas
alane - alone
alang - along
alas - sadly
amaist - almost
amang - among

ambrie - cupboard
an - if
an' - and
ance - once
ane - one
ane - own (their)
aneath - beneath
anent - concerning
anes - ones
aneugh - enough
anither - another
a's - all is
ase - ash
ashet - serving dish
asklent - squint
aspar - spread out
aster - stirring
atains - at once
athart - athwart (contradictory)
athole - hawk
at tour - moreover
atweel - of course
aught - possession
aughteen - eighteen
aughtlins - in any way
auld - old
auld reekie - Edinburgh (old smoky)

auld-warld - old-world
aumous - alms, (money or food given to the poor)
aumous-dish - begging bowl
ava - at all
awa - away
awald - doubled up
awauk - awake
awe - owe
awfu' - awful
awnie - bearded
awsome - frightful
ayont - beyond
ay - always

B

ba' - ball
babie - baby
babie clouts - baby clothes
backet - bucket
backit - backed
backlins - backwards
bade - asked
baggie - belly
baig'nets - bayonets
baillie - magistrate
bainie - bony
bairn - child / baby

baith - both
bakes - biscuits
ballats - ballads
balloch - mountain pass
bamboozle - confound, trick
ban - curse
ban' - bond
bane - bone
bang - effort
bannet - bonnet
bannock - round flat loaf, cake
barket - barked
barley-bree - whisky
barm - yeast
bartie - the devil
batts - colic
bauchles - old shoes
bauckie-bird - a bat, (flying bat)
baudrons - cat
bauk - rafter
bauld - bold
bawbee - halfpenny
bawk - untiled ridge
baws'nt - white
bawtie - dog
bear / bere - barley
bearded-bere - ripe barley

beas' - vermin
beastie - small animal
beb - drink
bedeen - immediately
beet - fan
beets - boots
befa' - befall
beft - beaten
begrutten - in tears
beik - bask
belang - belong
beld - bald
bellum - assault
bellys - bellows
belyve - quickly / at once
ben - mountain
ben - into, through, within
benison - blessing
bent - field
bere / bear - barley
bestead - provided
bethankit - Give God thanks, grace after a meal
beuk - book
beyont - beyond
bi - by / beside
bi crivens - Christ defend us
bicker (noun) - wooden dish

bicker (verb) - stagger
bide - stay
bield - shelter
bien - prosperous
big - build
biggin - cottage
biggit - built
bill - bull
billie - friend / companion
bing - heap
birk - birch
birken-shaw - small wood
birkie - fellow
birl - carouse
birnie - rough
birr - energy
birses - bristles
bit - place
bizz - bustle
black-bonnet - church elder
blastie - mischievous
blate - bashful
blather - bladder
blathrie - chatter
blatter - rattle
blaud - large quantity
blaw - blow, exaggerate

blawart - bluebell
blirt - weep / cry
blythe - gentle / kind
bocked - vomited
bogshaivle - distort
bonie - beautiful
bony - beautiful
boreas - the north wind
bosom - chest / breasts
bow-hough'd - bandy-legged
brachens - ferns
brae - slope, hillside
braid - broad
braid-claith - broad cloth
braird - first sprouting of corn / barley – etc
braik - harrow
braindg't - reeled
brainge - barge
brak - break
brander - gridiron (a frame of parallel bars)
brands - calf muscles
brang - bought
brankan - prancing
branks - halter (a strap or rope around the head of an animal)
brankie - gaudy / smart
brash - illness

brats - scraps
brattle - scamper / run
brattle - clatter / noisy
braw - beautiful / handsome
brawlie - heartily
braxie - dead sheep
breastie - breast
breastit - sprang / jumped
brechame - halter
breckan - fern
bree - juice, (whisky)
breeks - britches / trousers
brent - smooth, high
brent -new- brand-new
brig - bridge
briss - press
brither - brother
brock - badger
brogue - trick / fool
broo - broth
brose - oatmeal dish
browden - fond / like
brownie - spirit
browst - ale / beer
brugh - burgh
brulzie - brawl / fight
brunstane - brimstone

brunt - burned
brust - burst
buff - thump
bught - pen
bughtin-time - milking-time
buirdly - stoutly
buller - bubble
bumbazed - confused
bum - clock- beetle
bummin - humming
bummle - useless person
bung - fuddled / confused
bunker - window-seat
burdie - bird / girl
bure - bore
burn - stream / brook
burnewin - blacksmith
burr-thrissle - thistle
busk - dress
buskie - bushy
buskit - dressed
buss - bush
bussle - bustle
but an' ben - kitchen & parlour
butching - butchering
byke - hive / nest

C

ca' - call
cadger - hawker
caddie - carrier / bearer
caff - chaff
cairn - pile of stones
cairts - playing cards
calf-ward - calf-pen, (enclosure)
callant - a youth (boy)
caller - bracing / cold
callet - girlfriend
cangle - wrangle
cankert - ill tempered
canna - cannot
cannie - cautious / go easy
cannie - gentle
cantie - jolly / happy
cantraip - magic spell
cape-stane - coping stone
careerin' - rushing
care na - care not
carfuffle - disorder / argument
cark - anxious
carle - old man
carline - old woman
cartes - playing cards
castock - cabbage stem

caudron - cauldron
cauf - calf
cauk - chalk
cauld - cold
cavie - coop (hen)
causey - causeway / street
ceilidh - dance / gathering
chafts - chops
chancy - fortune
change-house - ale-house / pub
chantan - chanting
chanters - bagpipes
chap (noun) - liquid measure
chap (verb) - rap / knock
chapman - pedlar
chaup - stroke
cheek-for-chow – cheek-by-jowl
chiel - fellow / man
chimla - fireplace
chimla-lug - fireside
chirm - sing
chittering - shivering
chuck - dear
chuffie - fat-faced
cit - citizen
clachan - village (small)
claes - clothes

claith - cloth
clank (ie) - knock
clarty / clartie - dirty
clash - chatter
clashmaclavers - gossip
claught - seized
claut - clean
claver - clover
clavers - tales / stories
cleed - clothe
cleek - clutch
cleekit - linked arms
cleuch - ravine
clink - coin / money
clinkin - jerking
clinkumbell - bell-ringer
clinty - stony
clips - shears
clash-ma-claver – nonsense
cloot - hoof
clout - patch
cluds - clouds
coft - bought
cog - wooden cup
commaun - command
coman - coming
comely - pleasing

cood - cud
coof - idiot / fool
cookit - hid
coor - cover
cooser - stallion
coost - cast
corbie - crow
core - crowd
corn't - fed with oats
cotter - cottage-dweller (someone who lives in a cottage)
couthie - aggreeable / pleasant
cowe - scare / frighten
cowpit - stumbled
cowslip - yellow flowers
crabbit - miserable / negative
crack - conversation
craft - croft
craig - rock
craigie - throat
crambo-jingle - rhymes
cranks - creaking
cranreuch - hoar-frost
crap - crop
craw - crow
creel - basket / confusion
creeshie - greasy

cronie - friend
croon - hum
crouchie - hunchbacked
crouse - merry
crowdie - porridge
crowl - crawl
crummie - cow
crummock - crooked staff
crump - crisp
cry - tell
culzie - flatter
cuif - idiot / fool
cun - earn
curch - kerchief
curmurring - commotion
curn - parcel
curple - buttocks
cutled - courted
cutty - short

D

dab - peck / pierce
daez't - bewildered
daffin - merriment
dail - plank
daidlin - waddling
daimen-icker - occasional ear of corn

dam - pent up water
dams - game of draughts
damn'd haet - damn all
dang - pushed / knocked
darg - work
darger - casual laborer
darklin - dark
daud - pelt
daunder - stroll / walk
daunton - subdue
daur - dare
daurt - dared
daut - fondle / pet
daver - wander aimlessly
dawd - lump
dawt - caress
dawin - dawning
dearthfu' - expensive
deave - deafen
defac'd - defaced
Deil - Devil
deleerit - delirious
delvin - digging
deray - disorder
dern - hidden
descrive - describe
deuk - duck

deval - descend
diddle - move quickly
differ - quarrel / dispute
dight - wipe / clean
dink - trim
dinmont - two year old sheep
dinna - don't
dint - affection
dirk - short dagger
dizzen - dozen
docht - dared
dochter - daughter
doit - small copper coin
doited - muddled
donsie - self important
doo - dove
dool - sorrow
douce - prudent / grave
douk - duck
doup - backside
dou / doo - dove
douk - dip / bathe
dour - sullen / unhappy
dow - can
dowff - dismal
downa - cannot
doxy - lover / suitor

doylt - stupid
doytin - doddering
draigl't - draggled / unkempt
drants - long prayers
drap - drop
draunting - drawling
dree - suffer
dreeping - dripping
dreigh - tedious
driddle - saunter / walk slow
drod - prick
droddum - backside / bum
droukit - drenched / soaked
drouth - thirst
drucken - drunken
drum - hillock / ridge
drumlie - muddy
drummock - oatmeal & water
drunt - bad mood
dub - puddle
duddies - ragged old clothes
dunt - hit / strike a blow
durk - dirk / short dagger
dusht - pushed / thrown
dwaum - swoon / feint
dyke - wall / dry stone wall
dynie - tremble

dyvor - Bankrupt

E

ear' - early
eard - earth
eastlin - eastern
e'ebrie - eyebrow
e'e - eye
een - eyes
e'en - even
e'enin - evening
eenou - immediately
eerie - strange / frightening
efface - erase
eggle - urge on
eke - also
eild - old age
elbuck - elbow
eldritch - unearthly
elekit - elected
eller - church elder
en' - end
eneugh - enough
enow - enough
erselins - backwards
esthler - carved stone
etter - fester

ettercap - spider
ettle - aim
even'd - compare
evermair - evermore
evite - shun
expeckit - expected
eydent - diligent

F

fa' - fall / to get / lot
fab - trick
faddom - fathom
fae - from / foe / enemy
faem - foam
faiket - let off / excused
fail - turf
fain - affectionate / fond
fair-fa' - welcome / good luck
fairin - present / reward
fairly - certainly
fairmers - farmers
fait - neat
faize - annoy / upset
fan - found
fand - found (past tense)
fank - sheep pen / rope coil
fankle - tangle

fantoush - flashy
farden - farthing
farl - scone / small oatcake
fash - trouble / irritate
fasht - troubled / bothered
Fasten-ee'ne - Shrove Tuesday
fat - what
fatt'rills - ribbons
fauld - fold
faun - fallen
faur - far
faur back - long ago
fause - false
faut - fault
fawsont - seemly
feal - field
fear't - frightened
fecht - fight
feck - majority / the bulk
fecket - waistcoat
feckless - weak
feerie - sturdy
feide - fued
feil - many
feirrie - lusty
fell - deadly
felly - relentless

fent - garment opening
ferlie - wonder / marvel
fernyer - last year
fetter - bind / chain
fettle - condition
fey - fated
fickle - changeable
fidgin-fain - restless
fiel - comfortable
fient - devilish
fier - well / friend
findy - substantial
fissle - tingle
fit - foot
flacht - handful
flait / flate - scolded
flawgaires - whimsies
fleesh - fleece
fleg - frighten
flesher - butcher
fletherin - flattering
fley'd - frightened
flichtering - fluttering
flinders - shreds
flinty - hard
fliskit - fretted
flit - move

fluther - hurry
flyte - scold
fodgel - plump
fon - fond
Foorsday - Thursday
for a' that - not withstanding
foraye - forever
Forfairn - worn out
forfouchen - exhausted
forgather - meet
forker - earwig
forleet - forsake
fou - drunk / full
foughten - troubled
fouth - plenty
frae - from
frammle - gobble
frist - trust
fu' - drunk / full
fud - backside (short tail)
fushion - vigour / spirit
fusionless - spiritless / weak
fustit - decayed
fyke - fidget
fyled - soiled / fouled

G

gab - talk / mouth
gae - go
gadsman - ploughboy
gallants - splendid men
gan - begun
gane - gone
gang - go
gangrel - vagrant
gar - make
gars - makes
gash - respectable
gat - got
gate - road
gath'rin - gathering
gaud - went
gauger - exciseman
gaun - going
gawky - akward
gawsie - jolly / buxom
gear - belongings
gentie - graceful
genty - trim / elegent
get - child / offspring
ghaist - ghost
gie - give
gif - if
gilpey - young woman

gin - against
girn - grin
girnal - meal chest
grin - snarl
glaikit - foolish
glaum'd - snatched
glen - valley
gloaming - twilight
glunch - frown
gowan - daisy
gowd - gold
gowden - golden
gowdie - head
gracefu' - graceful
graff - grave
graith - harness
grat - wept / cried
gree - prize
greet - weep
grippit - mean
grozet - gooseberry
gropsy - glutton
guddle - mess / mangle
gude - god
guid - good
guidman - master of the house

guid-willie waught – cup of kindness / goodwill drink
gully - large knife
gumlie - muddy
gumption - commonsense
gurlie - rough
gut-scraper - fiddler
gyte - insane / mad

H

ha' - Hall
habber - stutter
haddie - Haddock (fish)
haddin - piossesion
hadna - had not
hae - have
haerst - harvest
haffet - lock of hair
hafflins - halfway
hag - moss
hain - spare
hald - hold
hale - fit / hearty
hallow mass - all Saints day
hame - home
han - hand
hand-wal'd - hand picked

hankers - desires
hap - wrap
harigals - entrails
harkit - listened
hash - oaf / idiot
haster - perplex
haud - hold
hauffet - temple
haughs - hollows
haurl - drag
havins - manners
hear'st - do you hear
hee - call
heeze - raise
hen-shin'd - bow-legged
here awa - here about / near
heugh - crag
hinderlets - hind parts
hindmost - last
hing - hang
hinny - honey
hirplin - limping
hizzie - hussy / slag
hoar - frost
hoast - cough
hool - the husk
hornie - devil

houlet - owl
housal - household
hov'd - swollen
howdie - midwife
howe - hollow / glen
howk - dig
hunkers - haunches
hurdies - buttocks
hure - whore
hurl - throw / crash

I

Icker - ear of corn
ier-oe - great grandchild
ilk - each
ilka - every
ill-deedy - mischievous
ill-willy - ill-natured
ingle - fireplace
ingle-gleede - blazing fireside
ingle-lowe - fire light
intermix'd - intermixed
inviolate's - untouched
ither - other
izles - embers

J

Jad - old horse
jag - pin prick
jauk - daily
jaup - splash
jaw - insolent talk
jawpish - tricky
jimplly - neatly
jinglan - jingling
jink - dodge
jo - sweetheart
jockey-coat - overcoat
jocteleg - clasp knife
jouk - dodge
jow - swing
jumpit - jumped

K

kae - jackdaw (bird)
kail - cabbage
kail-whittle - cabbage knife
kail-yard - cabbage patch
kain - rents in kind
kame - comb
katy-handit - left handed
kebars - rafters
kebbuck - cheese

keek - peep / look
keekin' glass - mirror
keel - chalk
keepit - kept
kelpies - water spirits
ken - know
ken't - knew
kenspeckle - easily recognized
ket - fleece
kiaugh - anxiety / worry
kinch - noose
kintra - country
kirk - church
kirn - harvest supper
kirsen - chisten
kiss caups - pledge friendship
kist - chest
kith - acquaintance / friend
kittle (adj) - difficult
Kittle (noun) - tickle
knaggie - nobly
knap - smart blow
knapper - head
knoited - knocked
knowe - hillock
knurl - dwarf
kye - cow

kyte - belly

L

Lac'd - corseted
lade - load
lady-landers - ladybird
laggen - bottom of a dish
laigh - low
laiglen - milking pail / bucket
lairing - sinking
laith - loath / hate
lallan - lowland
lammas - August 1st / harvest
lammie - lamb
landlowper - vagabond / tramp
lane - lone
lang - long
lang syne - long ago
langsum - tedious / boring
lantron - lantern / light
laughan - laughing
laun - land
lave - remainder / rest
laverock - lark (bird)
law - hill
lawin - bill
lea' - leave

leal - loyal
lear - learning
lee-lang - live long
leesome - pleasant
leeve - live
leeze - bless
leister - spear
len' - lend
leugh - laugh
leuk - look
libbet - gelded / castrated
limmer - mistress
linket - skipped
linn - waterfall
lint - flax / linseed plant
lippen - trust
loan - lane
loof - palm
loon / loun - lad / roguish boy
loot - allow
loup / lowp - leap / jump
lov'd - loved
lov'st - loves
lowe - flame
lowse - loose
luckie - old woman
luesom - lovely

lug - ear
lugget - having ears
luggie - two handled cup
lum - chimney
luntin - smoking
lume - loom
lure - rather
lurve - love
lyart - grey / withered / old
lye - lie

M

mae - more
Mahoun - Devil
maik - equal
mair - more
maist - most
maister - master
mak - make
mak'sna - matters not
mantie - gown
mang - among
manna - food from God
manteel - mantle
mantling - foaming
maskin pat - tea pot
maught - might

maukin - hare
maun - must
maunna - must not
maut - malt
mavis - thrush / bird
mere / meare - mare / female horse
meikle - large
mein - look / demeanour
men' - mend
mense - sense / tact
menseless - senseless
menzie - follower
merk - old Scottish coin
mess John - church minister
middin - dunghill / scrapheap
middlins - moderately
milkin' shiel - milking parlour
mim - meek
mim mou'd - gently spoken
min' - remember
mind - bear in mind
mindna - forget
Minnie - mother
mirk - gloom
misca' - abuse
mishanter - mishap / accident
mislear'd - unmannerly / rude

mislippen - disappoint
mismarrow - mismatch
mistaen - mistaken
mith - might
mither - mother
moch - moist
monie - many
mony - many
moolin - crumb
mools - dust
moop - nibble
moosty - mouldy
mottle - dusty
mou' - mouth
moubit - mouthful
moudiwort - mole
muckle - great
muir - moor
mumpit - stupid
musing - thinking
muslin - kail- thin broth (soup)
mutchkin - English pint
mysel - myself

N

na' - not
nack - trick

nae - no
naebody - nobody
naething - nothing
naig - pony
naither - neither
nane - none
nappy - ale / beer
nar - near
nay - no / or rather
neebor - neighbor
needfu' - needful
needna - need not
negleck - neglect
neist - next
neth - below
neuk - corner
newlins - very lately
nicht - night
nick - small cut
nicket - cheated
niest - next
nieve - fist
niffer - exchange
nit - nut
nocht - nought
noddle - brain
norlan - northland

notour - notorious
nourice - nurse
nowte - cattle
nowther - neither

O

o'boot - gratis / free
ocht - aught
ochtlins - in the least
o'erhung - overhung
o'erlay - smock /dress
o'erword - chorus
onie - any
orra - extra
o't - of it
oughtlins - in the same degree
ouk - week
ourie - shivery
oursels - ourselves
out - owre- above
owre - over
owsen - oxen
owther - either
owthor - author
oxter - armpit

P

pack - intimate
paction - agreement
paidle (noun) - puddle
paidle (verb) - dawdle
painch - paunch / large belly paitrick- partridge (bird)
pang - cram
parishen - parish
parritch - porridge
pash - head
pat - pot
pattle - plough staff / stick
paughty - proud
pawkie - cunning
pechan - stomach
pechin - out of breath
peet mow - peat stack
peinge - whine
peltry - trash
penny fee - wages
penny wheep - small beer
pensfu' - conceited
philibeg - kilt
phoebus - Apollo / the sun
phraise - flatter
pickle - small quantity

pimpin - low / mean
pine - pain
pint stowp - pint measure
pit - put
plack - pennies
plackless - penniless
pleugh / plew - plough
plouk - pimple / spot
poacher court - Kirk Session
pock - pocket
poind - seized
pooch - pouch
pook - pluck
poortith - poverty
pou - pull
pouk - poke / jab
poupit - church pulpit
pouse - push
poussie - hare / cat
pouther - powder
pow - head
pownie - pony
pree'd - tasted
preen - pin
presses - cupboards
preeve - prove
prent - print

prief - proof
prigging - haggling
prostration - subservience
pu' - pull
pultrous - lecherous
pund - pound
pursie - small purse
pussie - hare
pyke - pick
pyle - grain
pystle - epistle

Q

quaite - quiet
quat - quit / give up
quauk - quake / shake
quey - cow
quine - young woman
quer - choir
quo - quoth / humorous

R

rade - rode
raff - plenty
raffan - hearty
ragweed - ragwort

raible - nonsense
rair - roar
ramfeezl'd - exhausted
ramgunshoch - rugged
rampin' - ragging / angry
ram stam - headlong
randie - riotous
rape- rope
raploch - home-spun
rarely - quickly
rash - rush
rattle - strike / hit
ratton - rat
raucle - fearless
raught - reached
raw - row
rax - stretch
ream - froth
reave - rob / steal
red / rede - advise
reek - smoke / smell
remead - remedy
reuth - pity
richt - right
rief - thieve
rig - ridge
rigs - ridges

riggin - roof
rin - run
ringle-ey'd - white-eyed
ripp - handful of corn
riskit - cracked
rither - rudder
rive - split
roon - round
roose - reputation
roosty - rusty
roving - walking / wandering
rowth - plenty
rowtin - lowing
rozet - rosin
rugh - rough
rullions - coarse shoes
rummle - stir about
rummlegumption - common sense
run - downright
rung - cudgel / weapon
runkle - wrinkle
ruth - sorrow
ryke - reach

S

sab - sob / cry loudly
sae - so

saebins - since it is so
saft - soft
saikless - innocent
sair (verb) - serve
sair (adj) - sore / hard
sairie - sorrowful
sall - shall
sark - shirt
saul - soul
saumont - salmon (fish)
saunt - saint
saut - salt
saw - sow / plant seeds
sax - six
scail - spill
scaith - injury
scantlins - scarcely
scar - scare
sconner - disgust / annoy
scraichin - screaming
scrievin - moving along
scrimpt - short / cut back
sculduggery - fornication
see'd - saw
seelfu - pleasant
seenle - seldom
see'st - do you see

session - court
set - start
shachl't - distorted
shanks - legs
shanna - shall not
shaul - shallow
shavie - trick / prank
shaw (noun) - woodland
shaw (verb) - show
shawpit - shelled
shaws - stalks
sheugh - ditch
sheuk - shook
shiel - shed
shool - shovel
shoon - shoes
shot - sort
shouldna - should not
shouther - sholder
sic / sik - such
sicker - steady
sidelins - sideways
siller - silver
simmer - summer
sin - since
sirple - sip
skaith- damage / mark

skeigh - skittish / nervous
skellum - rogue
skelpin - rushing
skilly - skillful
skinking - watery
skinklin - small
skirl - shriek
sklent - side-look
skrimmish - skirmish / fight
skurrivaig - vagabond / tramp
skyre - shine
skyte - lash
slade - slid
slae - sloe
slaik - lick
slap - gap
slaw - slow
slee - sly
sleekit - sleek/ cunning
sloken - slake / quench thirst
sma' - small
smack - kiss
smawly - small
smeddum - powder / malt dust
smeek - smoke
smiddie / smiddy - blacksmith
smirtle - shy smile

smoor - smother
smurr - drizzle
smytrie - group / collection
snakin - sneering
snash - abuse
snaw - snow
sned - cut off
snell - sharp
sneshin - snuff
snick - latch
snirtle - snigger
snool - snub
snowkit - snuffed
sodger - soldier
sole - sill
sonnet - song
sonsie - pleasant
soom - swim
soor - sour
souk - suck
souple - supple
souter - cobbler / shoe maker
sowp - spoonful
sowther - solder
spae - foretell
spair - spare
spak - spoke

spean - wean / get used to
speat - spate
speel - climb
speet - skewer
speir - ask
spelder - tear apart
spence - parlour
spleuchan - tobacco pouch
splore - frolic / carousal
sprattle - scramble
spreckle - speckled
spirritie - full of spirits
sprush - dressed up
spunk - spirit
spunkie - will o' the wisp
squattle - squat
stab - stake (wooden)
Stacher - stagger
stan' - stand
stane - stone
stang - sting
stank - pool
stap - stop
stapple - stopper
stark - strong
staumrel - silly
staw - sicken

stechin - cramming
steek - stitch
steer - stir
steeve - compact
stell - still
stent - duty
steyest - steepest
stibble - stubble
stickit - stuck
stimpart - quarter measure
stirk - young cow
stoiter - stumble
stotter - stagger
stoun / stown - stolen
stounds - aches
stoure - dust / battle
stowp - cup
strae - straw
stak - stuck
staike - stroke
stramash - argument / fight
strang - strong
straught - straight
stravaugin - roaming
streekit - stretched
streen - last night
striddle - straddle

studdie - anvil
stumle - stumble
stump - stop / halt
stumpie - stout
sturt - fret / worry
sucker - sugar
sugh - sigh
sumph - blockhead / idiot
sune - soon
suthron - southern
swall'd - swelled
swain - suitor / lover
swally - swallow / drink
swankie - fine fellow
swarf - to swoon
swat - sweat
swatch - sample / little bit
swats - light beer
swee - over
sweer - lazy
swith - get away
swither - hesitate
swoor - swore
syne - since / then

T

tack - lease

tackets - shoe-nails
tae - toe
taen - taken
taigle - hinder
taikle - tackle
tairge - target
taisle - tassel
tak - take
tald - told
tangs - tongs
tap - top
tapetless - thoughtless
tapsalteerie - topsy-turvy
tassie - cup
tauk - talk
tauld - told
teat - small quantity
ted - spread
teen - anger
tensum - ten together
tent (noun) - caution
tent (verb) - tend
tentie - careful
tentless - without a care
teugh - tough
teuk - took
thack - thatch

thae - those
thairm - intestines
thankit - thanked
thegither - together
thereanet - about that
thick - inmate
thieveless - forbidding
thiggin - begging
thir - these
thirl - thrill
tho' - although
thocht - thought
thole - endure
thon - you
thou'se - thou shalt
thowe - thaw
thrang (noun) - a crowd
thrang (verb) - busy
thrapple - throat
thrave - 24 sheaves of corn
thraw - twist
threed - thread
threep - maintain
threesum - three together
threteen - thirteen
thretty - thirsty
thrist - thirst

thrissle - thistle
throu'ther - confused
thumpit - thumped
thurst - thrust
thysel - thyself / yourself
timmer - timber
timmer-tuned - unmusical
tip / toop - ram (tup) / a sheep
tipper - taiper- teeter
tine - lose
tinkler - tinker / tramp
tint - lost
tippence - two pence
tippenny - two-penny beer
tir - tap
'tis - it is
tither - other
tittle - whisper
tocher - marriage bonds
tod - fox
Tod Lowrie - fox
too fa' - lean-to
toom - empty
tother - other
toun - farmland
towsie/tousie - shaggy
tow - rope

towsing - handling
towmound - twelve-month
toy - cap
tozie - tipsy
traiket - disordered
trashtrie - rubbish
trepan - ensnare
trig - neat
trowth - trust
tryste - appointment
try't - tried
tuffle - ruffle
tulzie - quarrel
tummle - tumble
tummler - cup / glass
tunefu' - tuneful
ture - tore
turkasses - pincers
turn - task
turrs - turfs
twa / tway - two
'twad - would have
twahaund - between two
twal - twelve
twasum - two together
tween - between
tweesh - betwixt / between

twin - sepatate from
twine - twist
tyesday - Tuesday
tyke - dog
tyken - bed linen
tylie - slice of beef
tyest - entice

U

ulzie - oil
unchancy - dangerous
unco - strange / very
undeemous - inconceivable
undocht - silly
uneith - difficult
unfauld - unfold
unfeiry - inactive
unkend - unknown
unkin - unkind
unloosome - unlovely / ugly
unsicker - uncertain
unsneck - unlock
unweeting - unwittingly
uphaud - uphold
upo' - upon
upsides - equal to
upstan't - stood

uptack - understanding
usquebah - whisky

V

van - group
vauntie - proud
vera / verra - very
vernal - springtime
vernal - youthful
virl - ring
vittles - food
vively - clearly
vogie - conceited
vowt - vault / jump

W

wa' - wall
wab - web
wabster - weaver
wad - wager
wad - would
waddin' - wedding
wadna - would not
wae - woe /sorrow
weaness - sadness
waesucks - alas

wair'd - spent
wale - choice
walie - large
wame - belly
wan - won / one
wanchancie - dangerous
wanrestfu' - restless
wanruly - unruly
wanwordy - unworthy
wap - wrap
wappon - weapon
war - were
ware - worn
wark - work
warl' / warld - world
war's gear - worldly possesions
warlock-breef - magic spell
warl'y - worldly
warna - were not
warran - warrant
warse - worse
warsle - wrestle
wart - were it
wast - west
wat - wet
water-fit - mouth of the river
waud - wade

waugh - damp
waught - large dink
wauk - wake
waukrife - sleepless
waukit - calloused
waur - worse
wawlie - handsome
wean - child
weary fa' - plague upon
weason - gullet
wecht - weight
weed - clothes
weel - well
weel-hain'd - well-saved
weet - wet
westlin - westerly
wha - who
whae - who
whaizle - wheeze
whalpit - whelped / birthed
whang - slice
whan - when
whar - where
whase - whose
whaup - curlew / bird
whid - fib / move quickly
whigmaleeries - whimsical

whilk - which
whirligigums - useless things
whisht - silence
whitter - measure of liquor
whommilt - turned upside down
whun - basalt / volcanic rock
whunner - rattle
whup - whip
whyles - sometimes
wi' - with
wifie - wife
willyart - awkward
wimple (verb) - wind
wimplin - winding
winch - wench
winna - will not
winnins - earnings / winnings
winnock-bunker – window seat
win's - winds
wise-like - respectable
wiss - wish
written - knowledge
wonner - wonder
woo' - wool
woodie - gallows
wook - weak
wordy - worthy

wrack - vex / annoy
wraith - spirit
wrang - wrong
wran - wren / song bird
wright - carpenter
writer - lawyer
wud - wild
wuddie - rope
wull - will
wure - wore
wursum - putrid
wurtle - writhe / squirm
wyliecoat - flannel vest
wyle - entice / attract
wyss - wise
wyte - blame

Y

Yad - old mare
yaird - yard
yarrow - white flower
yauld - vigorous
yaumer - murmur
ye - you
ye'd - you would
ye'll - you will
yell - barren / empty

yellockin - squalling
yer - your
yersel - yourself
ye'se - ye shall / you shall
yestereen - last evening / night
yett - gate
yill - ale
yince - once
yird - earth
yirdit - buried
yokin - set to
yon - that
yonner - yonder
'yont - beyond
younker - youth
yowe - ewe / a sheep
yowie - lamb / young sheep

ABOUT THE AUTHOR

Alastair Turnbull walking "The West Highland Way"

Alastair Turnbull is a Scotsman and author of Non Fiction books. These books are usually on the subjects of **Scotland**, **Drinks & Drinking** and **Robert Burns**. These also happen to be three of Alastair's greatest passions in life - after his **wife** and two **daughters**.

Alastair lives in Scotland and has been self-employed for over 15 years in the conference, events and exhibition industry. Working as an Audio-visual technician he has travelled the globe working with a large variety of companies from pharmaceuticals to wind energy specialists, solicitors to potato farmers. If you have no idea what that actually means, just think of him as a corporate "roadie".

Alastair started his writing career with the web site:
www.TheDrinkingMansGuideToScotland.com

This site, which is still very much alive and well, was born after working at endless road shows and events with Scottish drinks producers. There was only so much information he could take in before it started to pour out onto web pages and then onto ebooks and magazines. After writing about the great drinks Scotland has to offer, he then started writing about his other two passions: Scotland and Robert Burns.

In his free time Alastair likes to spend time with his family and indulge his three passions. This usually involves him dragging them around yet another Distillery / Brewery / Winery / Cider Mill in Scotland, whilst telling them how this relates to Robert Burns work as an excise man.

His family doesn't always enjoy spending time with him.

A Little Extra…

Alastair's wife's maiden name is Christine Burns. Christine's fathers name was **Robert Burns**. He was a farmer from Ayrshire.

Christine & Alastair Turnbull

ALSO BY ALASTAIR TURNBULL

Robert Burns - Nature:

Robert Burns – Food & Drink

Robert Burns - Life

Robert Burns - Death

Robert Burns - Scotland

Toasts & Toasting – A Simple Guide to Great Toasts, Blessings & Graces

This book is a guide to making a toast, whether it is at a wedding, birthday, graduation, funeral, etc. It also looks at Blessings, Graces, toasting traditions and toasting folklore.

Alastair Turnbull also writes for the web site:

TheDrinkingMansGuideToScotland.com

Made in United States
North Haven, CT
05 February 2024